Robots

KINGFISHER

Kingfisher Publications Plc
New Penderel House,
283–288 High Holborn,
London WC1V 7HZ
www.kingfisherpub.com

First published by Kingfisher Publications Plc 2003
2 4 6 8 10 9 7 5 3
SBC/0904/PROSP/RNB(RNB)/140MA

A CIP catalogue record for this book is
available from the British Library.

ISBN 0 7534 0842 2

Senior editor: Belinda Weber
Designer: Peter Clayman
Picture manager: Cee Weston-Baker
Picture researcher: Rachael Swann
DTP coordinator: Sarah Pfitzner
Artwork archivists: Wendy Allison, Jenny Lord
Senior production controller: Nancy Roberts
Indexer: Chris Bernstein

Printed in China

Acknowledgements
The Publisher would like to thank the following for permission to reproduce their material. Every care has been taken to trace
copyright holders. However, if there have been unintentional omissions or failure to trace copyright holders, we apologise and
will, if informed, endeavour to make corrections in any future edition.
b = bottom, *c* = centre, *l* = left, *t* = top, *r* = right

Photographs: *cover*: Oscar Williams © 1997/ BBH Exhibits Inc. 6-7 *c* Sony/SDR-4X; 8-9 *l* Getty Images; *c* eMuu, Dr. Christoph Bartneck,
Technical University of Eindhoven; *br* Peter Menzel/Science Photo Library; 10-11 *bl* James King-Holmes/Science Photo Library; *br* Photo:
(Ingrid Friedl) Lufthansa Technik Skywash/Lufthansa, Putzmeister AG; *tr* Space and Naval Warfare Systems Center, San Diego;
12-13 *cl* © Randy Montoya, Sandia National Laboratories; *c* Robosaurus/Doug Malewicki, Monster Robot Inc., *tr* Coneyl Jay/Science Photo
Library; 14-15 *bl* Honda Asimo; *tr* Eriko Fugita/Reuters/Popperfoto; *c* Sam Ogden/Science Photo Library;16-17 *bl* Sony/AIBO ERS-220;
tr © Dr. Gavin Miller SnakeRobots.com, Copyright 2000; *r* BBH Exhibits Inc./Oscar Williams; 18-19 *cl* Richard Bachmann, Gabriel Nelson
and Roger Quinn at Case Western Reserve University; *bc* MIT, Bruce Frisch/Science Photo Library; *tr* Sarcos; 20-21 *tr* PA photos/Sony;
br PA photos; *tr, bl* TM Robotics (Europe) Ltd/Toshiba; 22-23 *bc* Associated Press; *bl* MIT Media Lab, Getty Images; *tr* NASA/Carnegie Mellon
University, Science Photo Library; 24-25 *bl* modelluboot@t-online.de (Norbert Brüggen); *c* Getty Images; *tr* Associated Press;
26-27 *bl* NASA/Science Photo Library; *tr* NASA/Science Photo Library; *br* Media Resource Center NASA/ Lyndon B. Johnson Space Center;
28-29 *tr* Courtesy of the School of Mechanical Engineering, The University of Western Australia; *b* Louisianna State University;
cr © Ron Sanford/CORBIS; *tl* Digital Vision; 30-31 *tc* PaPeRo/© NEC Corporation 2001-2003; *cl* © Roger Ressmeyer/Corbis; *br* Electric
handout/Reuters/Popperfoto; 32-33 *bl* Spencer Grant/Science Photo Library; *br* Roy Garner/Rex Features; *tr* CRASAR™/www.crasar.org;
34-35 *bl* Associated Press; *c* © Cynthia's Bar and Restaurant; *tr* Associated Press; 36-37 *bc* Peter Menzel/Science Photo Library;
cl r. AeroVironment Inc.; *tr* www.edwards.af/Edwards Air Force Base; 38-39 Peter Menzel/Science Photo Library;
40-41 *bl* Tri-Star for *Short Circuit*/Kobal; *bl* Sautelet, Jerrican /Science Photo Library; *tr* AAR Productions/Kobal.
Short Circuit Tri-Star Pictures; *Return of the Jedi* Lucasfilm; *Doctor Who* BBC TV

Commissioned photography on pages 42–47 by Andy Crawford.
Thank you to models Eleanor Davis, Lewis Manu, Daniel Newton, Lucy Newton, Nikolas Omilana and Olivia Omilana.

Kingfisher Young Knowledge

Robots

Clive Gifford

Contents

What is a robot?

Robots are amazing machines that can work on their own. They can go into many places – from space to deep underwater.

Eyes, ears, mouth

Robots collect information about the world using devices called sensors. This Sony robot has sensors which record sound, and cameras which capture pictures.

sensors – devices which give a robot information about its surroundings

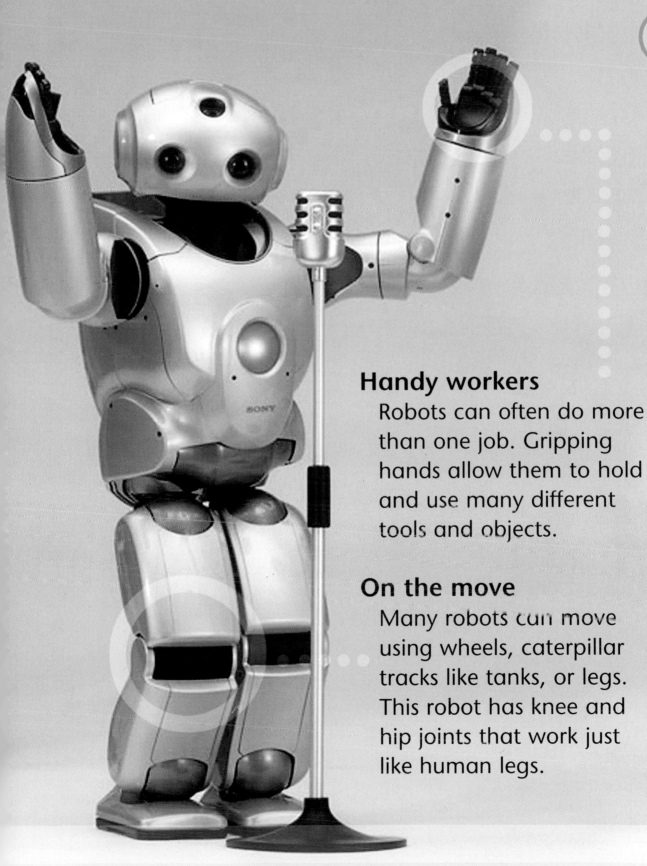

Handy workers

Robots can often do more than one job. Gripping hands allow them to hold and use many different tools and objects.

On the move

Many robots can move using wheels, caterpillar tracks like tanks, or legs. This robot has knee and hip joints that work just like human legs.

Robot controllers

Controllers are a robot's brain. They make decisions for the robot and operate all of its parts. Robot controllers are usually computers.

Fast thinkers

Computers make decisions very quickly. *Deep Junior* can think through three million chess moves every second. Here, it is playing the former World Chess champion, Garry Kasparov.

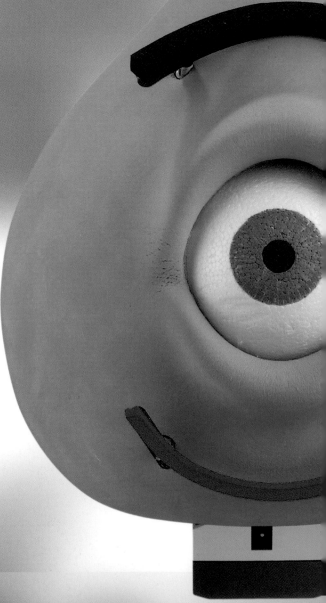

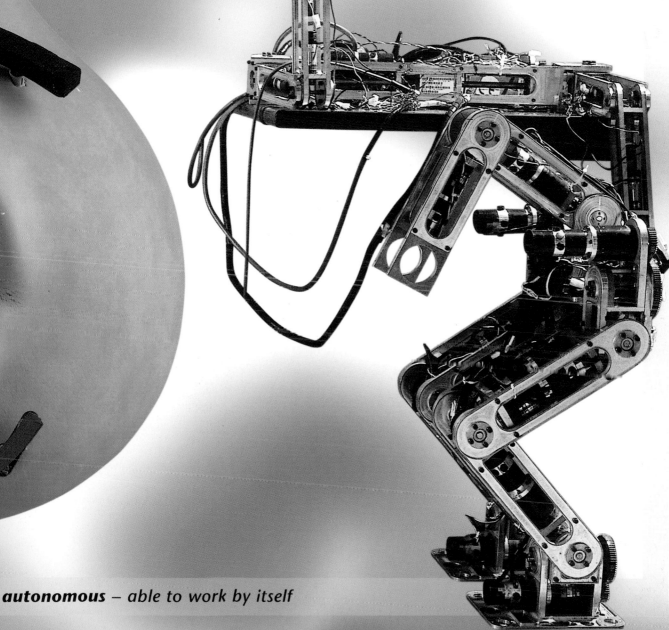

Showing emotion

This robot is called *eMuu*. It interacts with people and can show many different expressions including happiness, anger and sadness.

Learning to walk

Some robots are controlled directly by people. Others are able to work by themselves. This autonomous robot from Japan is teaching itself to walk.

autonomous – *able to work by itself*

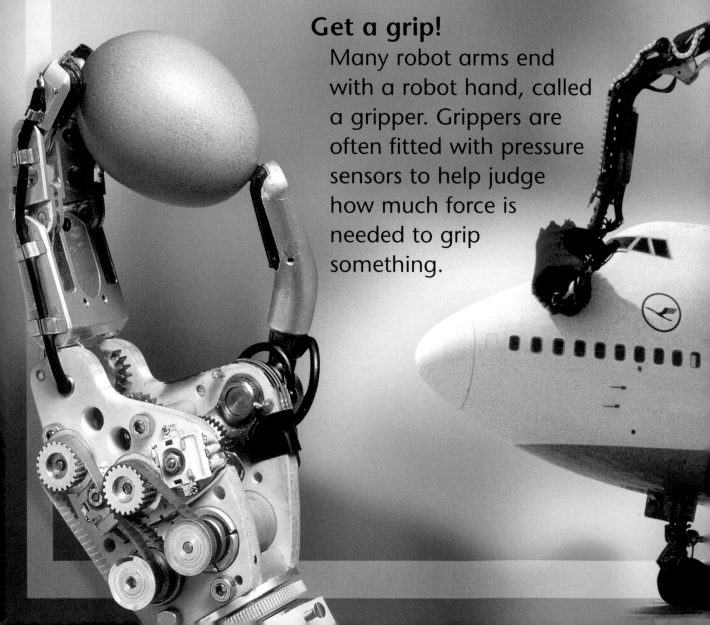

Robot **arms**

Robot arms are the most popular type of robot. They have joints so the arm can move in many different directions, just like a human arm.

Get a grip!

Many robot arms end with a robot hand, called a gripper. Grippers are often fitted with pressure sensors to help judge how much force is needed to grip something.

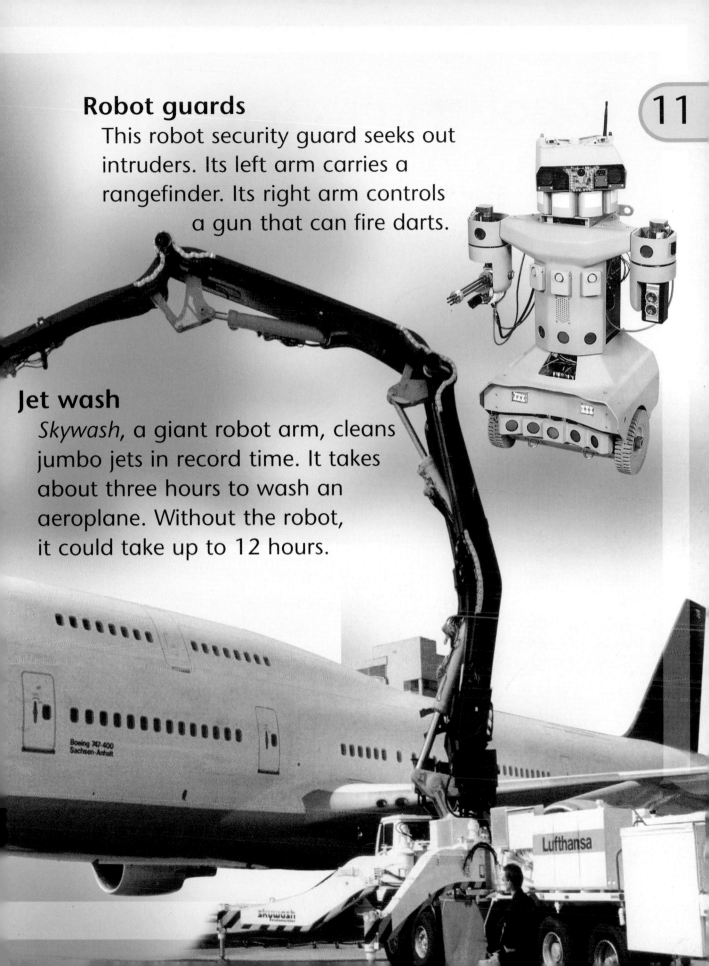

Robot guards

This robot security guard seeks out intruders. Its left arm carries a rangefinder. Its right arm controls a gun that can fire darts.

Jet wash

Skywash, a giant robot arm, cleans jumbo jets in record time. It takes about three hours to wash an aeroplane. Without the robot, it could take up to 12 hours.

Robots **big and small**

Robots come in many shapes and sizes. The largest are many metres high and weigh thousands of kilograms. Different sized robots use different power systems to move their parts.

Mighty monster

Robosaurus is a huge car-crushing monster. It uses hydraulic power to lift and destroy cars, trucks and even aeroplanes!

Marvellous *MARV*

MARV is a moving robot that is so small it can sit on a coin! Its tiny electric motor is powered by watch batteries. *MARV* can only move at a speed of 50 centimetres a minute.

hydraulic power – *a power system using liquids to gene*

Shrinking small

One day, robots may become so small they will be able to travel inside our bodies! Robots might travel through our veins, cleaning and repairing them.

Humanoid robots

People are fascinated by machines which look and act just like them. Scientists are building humanoid robots that can carry out a wide range of skills.

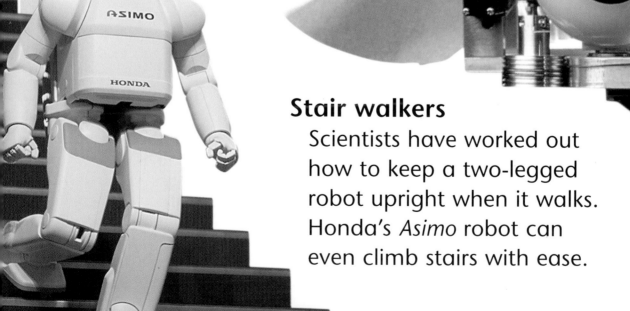

Stair walkers

Scientists have worked out how to keep a two-legged robot upright when it walks. Honda's *Asimo* robot can even climb stairs with ease.

Fancy a ride?

This humanoid robot from Asia acts as a rickshaw driver, pulling people around. It is powered by motors in its head and chest.

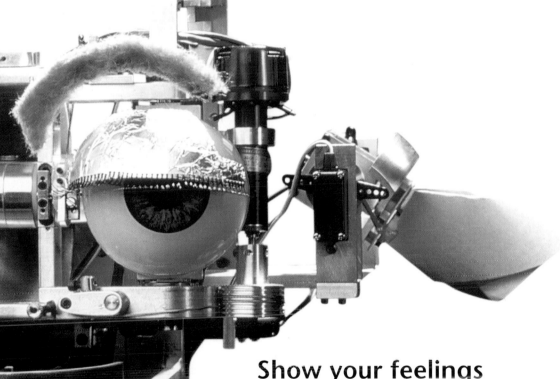

Show your feelings

Kismet is one of the few robots able to show facial expressions. Its mouth, eyelids, eyebrows and eyes all move to show expressions such as fear, happiness, disgust, interest and surprise.

humanoid – *looking or acting like a person*

Robot animals

Some robots look like animals. This may be to make an exhibition more fun or to make animatronic models for movies. Scientists also borrow ideas from animals to make robots move smoothly.

Snakes alive

Snakes move by sliding their bodies across the ground. This robot *S5* snake can slide through pipes and other cramped spaces.

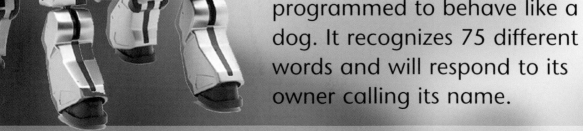

A new best friend

Sony's *AIBO ERS-220* is a new mobile robot which has been programmed to behave like a dog. It recognizes 75 different words and will respond to its owner calling its name.

animatronic – a model that uses computers and robotics to bring it to life

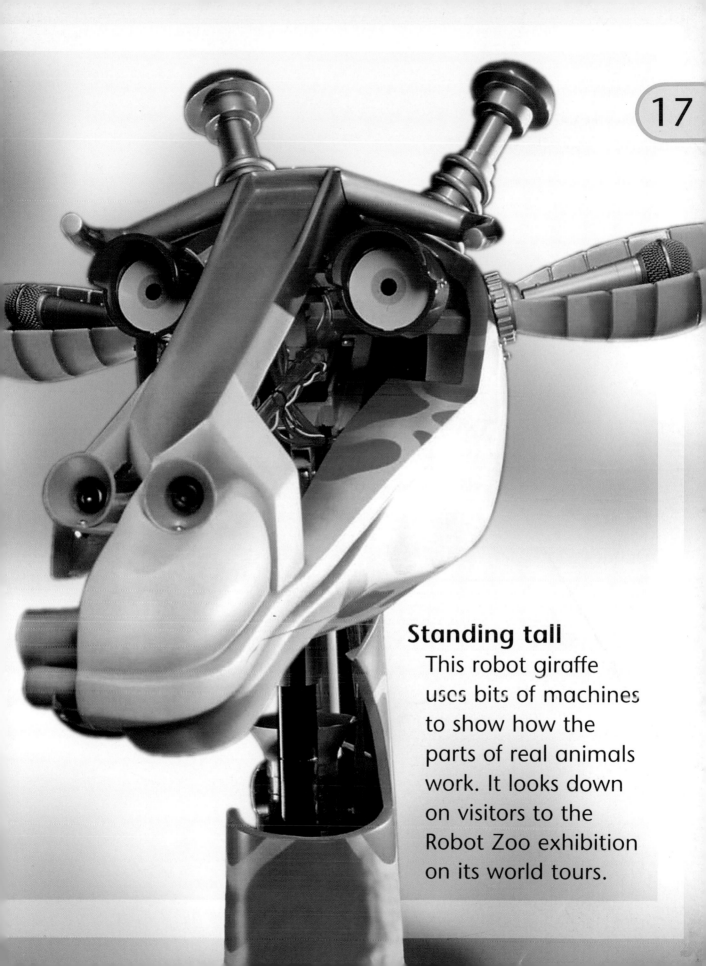

Standing tall

This robot giraffe uses bits of machines to show how the parts of real animals work. It looks down on visitors to the Robot Zoo exhibition on its world tours.

Robot insects

Insects are very successful creatures that can live in many different places. Robot-makers have copied some insects to help them build robots that can work in extreme conditions.

Robo-roach!

Ajax is designed to look like a cockroach. Its front legs each have five joints and the robot can stay balanced on just three of its six legs.

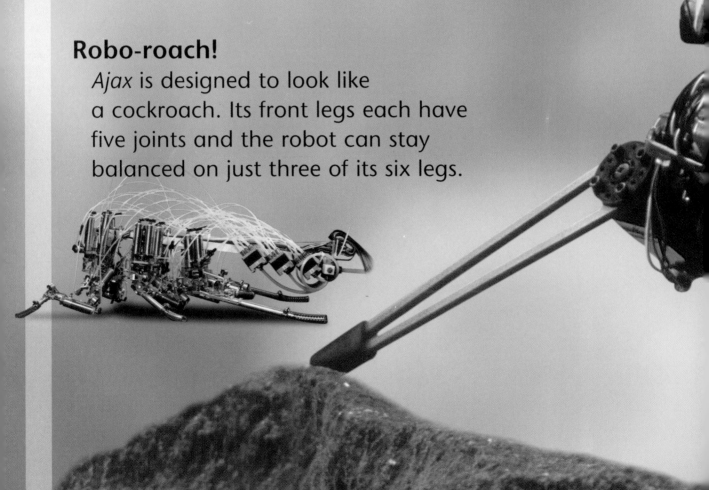

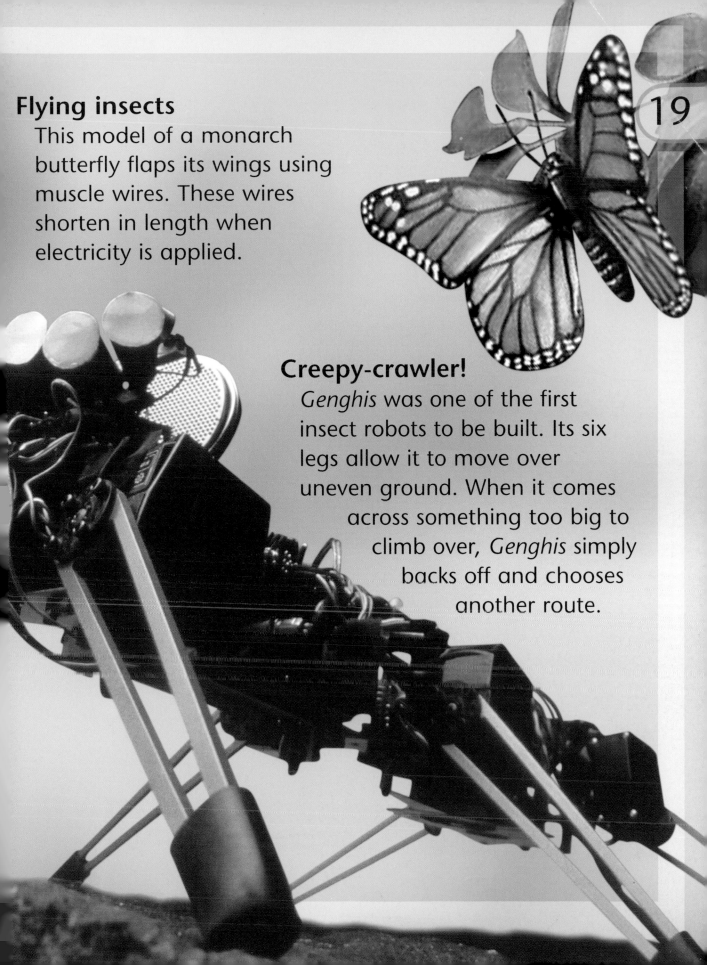

Flying insects

This model of a monarch butterfly flaps its wings using muscle wires. These wires shorten in length when electricity is applied.

Creepy-crawler!

Genghis was one of the first insect robots to be built. Its six legs allow it to move over uneven ground. When it comes across something too big to climb over, *Genghis* simply backs off and chooses another route.

Having fun

Playing sports is lots of fun for people, but for robots it is a big test of their abilities. Robots need to be able to make quick decisions and move their parts rapidly to play sports.

Playing volleyball

These Japanese test robots are learning to play volleyball. Each robot uses cameras to track the path of the ball and times the movement of its joints to meet the ball in mid-air.

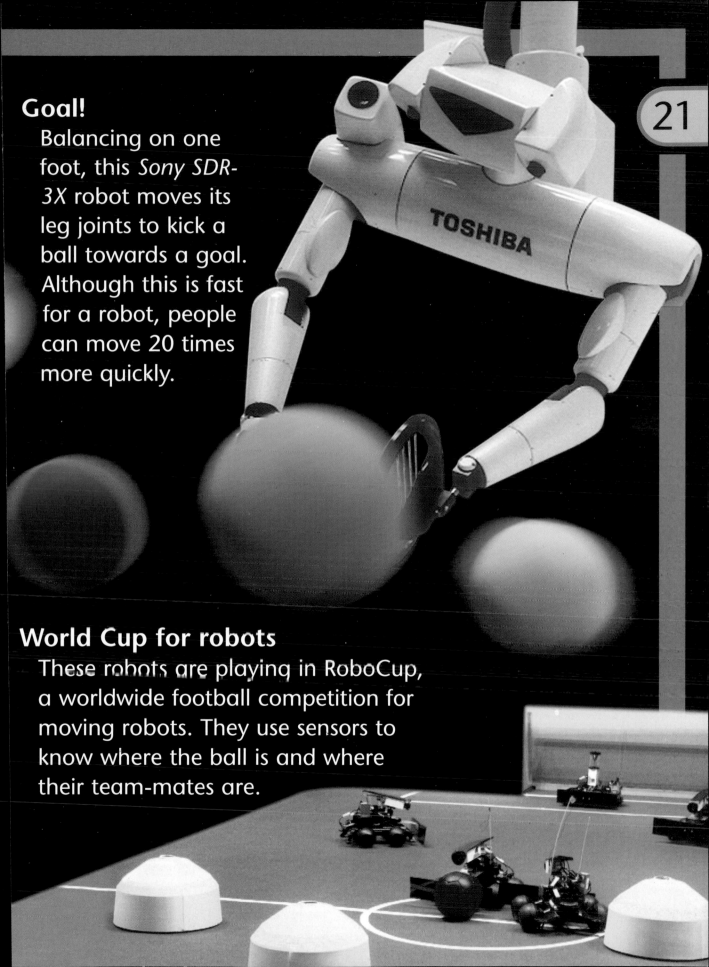

Goal!

Balancing on one foot, this *Sony SDR-3X* robot moves its leg joints to kick a ball towards a goal. Although this is fast for a robot, people can move 20 times more quickly.

World Cup for robots

These robots are playing in RoboCup, a worldwide football competition for moving robots. They use sensors to know where the ball is and where their team-mates are.

Robot explorers

Robots can be built to explore places too dangerous for people to visit. They can take pictures, and send back useful information, without putting people at risk.

Robo reporter

This test robot, *Afghan Explorer*, may one day visit war zones. Working as a war reporter, it could send pictures and interviews back to a TV studio in a safer place.

Into the volcano

This eight-legged robot is called *Dante II*. It can climb into the crater of a red-hot volcano to collect gas samples and take photos with its eight cameras.

Hot and cold worker

Nomad Rover is the size of a small car. It has trekked through hot deserts and icy lands all on its own, collecting information for scientists at home. In Antarctica, it discovered five meteorites.

meteorite – *a piece of rock or metal that has fallen to earth from space*

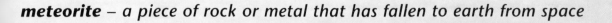

Underwater robots

Many robots work underwater. They map the ocean floor, monitor sea life or find sunken wrecks. Robots can travel deep underwater far more easily than people.

Unmanned submarine

Robots can stay underwater for many days at a time. They can travel hundreds of kilometres exploring the oceans.

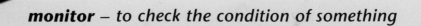

monitor – to check the condition of something

Deep-sea explorer

Robots like *Deep Drone* can travel to the ocean floor and help recover crashed aircraft or sunken ships. *Deep Drone* can travel around 40 times deeper than unprotected human divers.

Robot jellyfish

Some underwater robots are modelled on real sea creatures. This robot jellyfish has a small electric motor which makes it rise and fall in the water just like the real thing.

unmanned – *without people on-board*

Robots in space

Astronauts need special equipment to survive in space. Robots do not need air, water or food. They can work on distant planets keeping in touch with Earth by radio signals.

Photos in space

Aercam Sprint robot
can zoom around the
outside of a Space Shuttle
or a space station. The
beachball-sized robot
sends images back
to the astronauts inside
the spacecraft.

Robot astronauts

Robonaut is a test robot
built by NASA to work
as a construction worker
in space. It has two robot
arms that can grip and
use a range of tools.

Mission to Mars

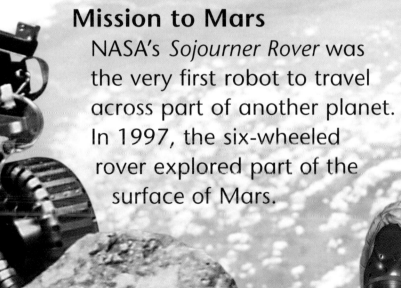

NASA's *Sojourner Rover* was
the very first robot to travel
across part of another planet.
In 1997, the six-wheeled
rover explored part of the
surface of Mars.

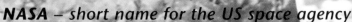

NASA – *short name for the US space agency*

Farm **robots**

Farming is hard work. Robots can help by doing some of the boring tasks that take up time. Farm robots can handle small plants, help at harvest or scare away pests.

Chasing birds

Scarebot is a robot that patrols catfish ponds in the United States. Its sudden movements scare away pelicans and other birds hoping for a fish supper!

programmed – *giving a computer or robot a list of instructions to perform*

Shear magic!
This robot from Australia has been programmed to shear the wool off a sheep. It can keep repeating the task, without getting tired.

Robots at home

Robots are coming home. The latest robots are doing useful jobs around the house. Home robots need to know their way around a house and be able to communicate with their owners.

Ready for breakfast?

Robots cannot cook your meals yet, but they can carry it to you. Home robots often hold a map of the house in their memory. They also need sensors to know when household objects are in their way.

communicate – to send or receive a message

Home playmates

PaPeRos wander around the house looking for people to talk to. They can recognize 650 different words and phrases, and speak up to 3,000 words. They can even dance!

Beware of the dog

This robot guard dog patrols the house checking that everything is safe. If it spots anything wrong, it can take pictures and send them to the owner's mobile phone.

32 Rescue **robots**

Some robots can save lives. They do this by fighting fires, searching for survivors after disasters, or handling dangerous objects such as unexploded bombs.

Handling bombs

Bomb disposal robots can look at suspect packages with their cameras. They relay the information to someone at a safe distance.

suspect – something which may be wrong or dangerous

SEP 15 2001
11:25:01 PM

Access all areas

Packbot enters unknown areas to check for danger. In 2001, *Packbot* searched the wreckage of the World Trade Center, in New York for survivors.

Fighting fires

Robots can cope with more heat than people, and they do not need air to breathe. This makes them excellent fire-fighters, getting in close to put out a blaze.

At your service

Service robots are able to perform useful, repetitive, everyday tasks for people. They are willing workers and do not get bored when doing simple jobs over and over again.

Fill her up!

Filling your car with petrol can be a fiddly business, but not for this robot attendant. Its robot arm can find a car's petrol tank, and fill it up with the amount of petrol the driver chooses.

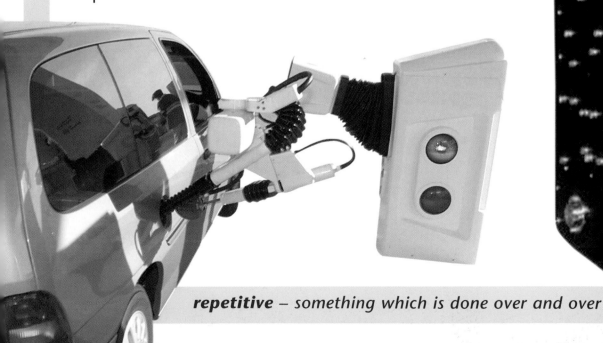

repetitive – something which is done over and over

Carry your bag

The *Intelecady* carries a bag of golf clubs around a course. The robot has a map of the course in its memory so it can avoid any bunkers or streams.

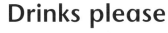

Drinks please

Cynthia is a robot bartender at work in London, England. *Cynthia*'s robot arms can select, grip and pour ingredients from bottles to mix customers one of 60 different drinks.

Spy robots

Human spies must be clever and sneaky. But robots can be built to get into places humans cannot, and send back information using radio signals. If spy robots are caught, they will not give away any secrets.

Mini-spy

Smaller robots can travel into places without being spotted. This flying robot is just 15 centimetres wide. It can fly for 30 minutes, powered by a tiny engine.

Hovering above

Cypher is a 1.8-metre-wide robot that can hover outside the windows of tall buildings. There, it can look and listen in on top secret meetings using microphones and cameras.

Watching you?

Roswell is a robot with 16 different sensors. Future spy robots may be able to identify people and follow them.

Robot doctors

Robots can work accurately for hours without error or getting tired. They make ideal assistants for human surgeons in hospital operations.

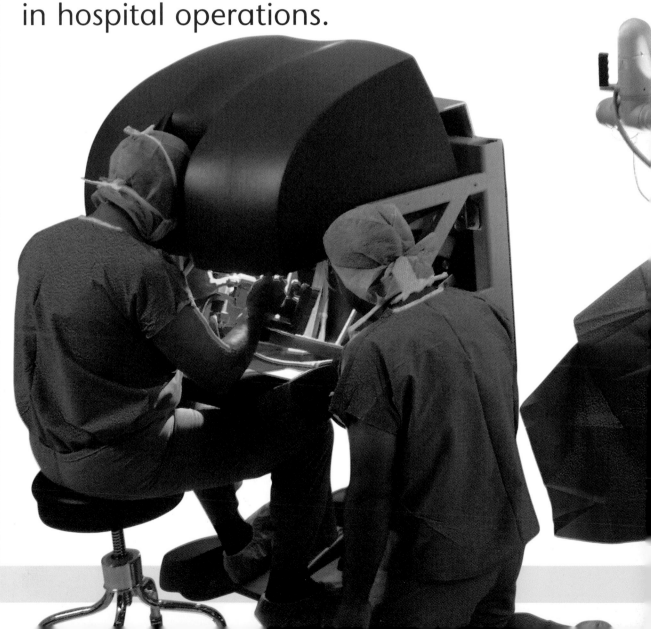

A steady hand

A human surgeon controls the *Da Vinci* robot while studying a magnified view of the operation. The robot's arms are fitted with surgical tools which perform the operation.

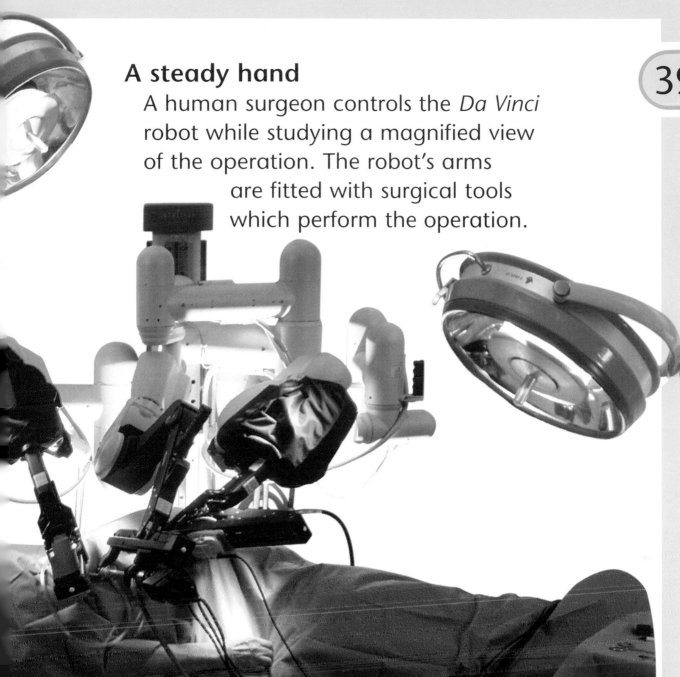

magnified – to make something look bigger

Sci-fi robots

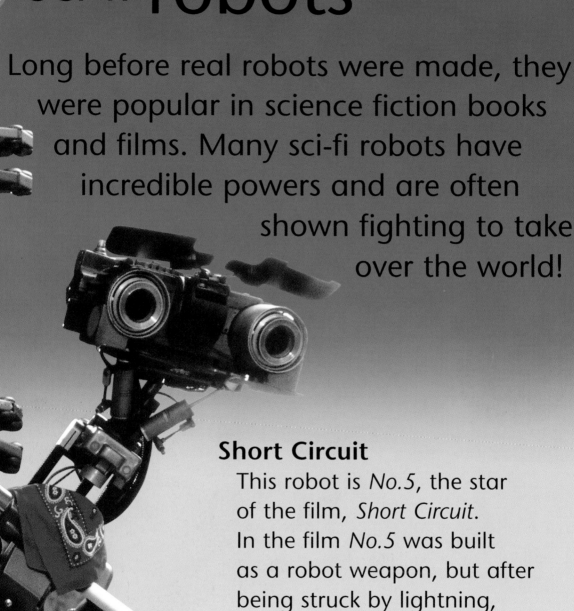

Long before real robots were made, they were popular in science fiction books and films. Many sci-fi robots have incredible powers and are often shown fighting to take over the world!

Short Circuit

This robot is *No.5*, the star of the film, *Short Circuit*. In the film *No.5* was built as a robot weapon, but after being struck by lightning, it refused to fight and started to learn and think for itself.

Exterminate!

Many sci-fi robots are shown as evil, including this *Dalek* from the *Doctor Who* TV show. Real robots are programmed by people, so are only as dangerous as people make them.

Robot actors

This animatronic model of *Yoda* is from the film *Return of the Jedi* from the *Star Wars* series. Its many electric motors allow it to make realistic movements.

42 Robot surprise!

Make a secret storage robot

Robots are super organized and find information very quickly. Make this robust robot storage box so that you can find your treasures whenever you need them, and keep your bedroom tidy!

You will need

- Shoe box
- Small box
- Poster paints
- Paint brush
- Scissors
- Cleaning cloth
- Glue
- Cardboard tubes
- Sweet wrappers
- Ping-pong balls
- Double-sided
  sticky tape
- Pipe cleaners

1

Paint the boxes, and cardboard tubes and leave to dry. Carefully cut off the two shorter ends of the shoe box lid along the fold line.

2

Using glue or double-sided sticky tape fix one edge of the lid to the shoe box, and press it down firmly. Cut two hand shapes from the cleaning cloth and attach a sweet wrapper or coloured paper to the ping-pong ball.

3

Use the smaller box as the robot's head, and decorate it with pipe cleaners. Cut the long cardboard tube in two and glue one cloth hand on each. Stick these on to the sides of the shoe box. Glue the other tubes on as feet, and the wrapped ball as a handle.

44 Moving as robots

Make a moving arm

Robots can be programmed to carry out many tasks. They can pick up things and move them around. This arm can pick up paper-clips.

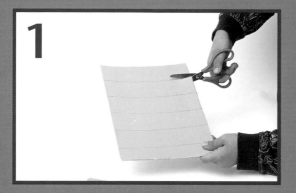

1

Using the scissors, carefully cut the thick card into strips. All the strips need to be the same length and width.

You will need

- Scissors
- 2 large sheets of thick card
- Paper-fasteners and -clips
- Double-sided tape or glue
- Small magnet

2

Make a crossover lattice of strips and join together with the paper-fasteners. You will need to use a paper-fastener in the middle of each strip, as well as at the ends.

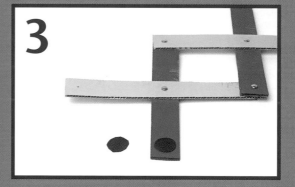

3

Take two small magnets and attach them to one end of the arm. By opening and closing the other end, you can use the arm to pick up paper-clips.

Walk like a robot

Very few robots can actually think for themselves. Most have to follow instructions. When you walk, your eyes show you where obstacles are and your brain works out how to avoid them. Here you can learn to move like a robot, just by following instructions.

Ask a friend to help you set up a maze using furniture. Find a blindfold, or close your eyes, but no peeking! Ask your friend to tell you how to walk through the maze without bumping into things. If the directions are wrong, you will hit the furniture!

46 Marvellous models

Make a model robot

Robots come in many shapes and sizes. Make a model robot out of empty cartons and boxes from your home. It can be any shape or size you like.

You will need
- Boxes
- Ping-pong balls
- Plastic cups
- Scissors
- Glue
- Cardboard tubes
- Silver foil
- Carton lid
- Pipe cleaners
- Thin card
- Sweet wrappers
- Coloured paper
- Sticky tape

Using glue, carefully stick silver foil around four of the cardboard tubes, and the boxes.

Cover another cardboard tube with coloured paper, and carefully cut into the ends, so they will sit flat.

Glue sweet wrappers or coloured paper on to an carton lid, then stick it to the big box.

Attach plastic cups on to one end of the big box. Stick a piece of card underneath, to help it stand.

5

6

Decorate the smaller box with painted ping-pong balls and pipe cleaners. Stick the arms on to your robot.

Open out the cut ends of the decorated cardboard tube and attach it to the head and body.

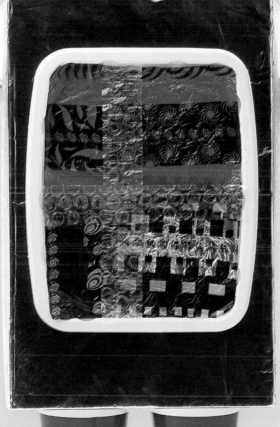

Index